Published by Smart Apple Media,
an imprint of Black Rabbit Books
P.O. Box 3263, Mankato, Minnesota 56002
www.blackrabbitbooks.com

Published by arrangement with
The Salariya Book Company Ltd

Cataloging-in-Publication Data is available
from the Library of Congress

Printed in the United States
At Corporate Graphics,
North Mankato, Minnesota

9 8 7 6 5 4 3 2 1

ISBN: 978-1-62588-341-4

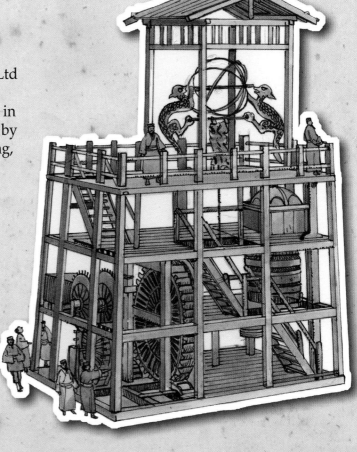

Illustrators: Mark Bergin
               David Antram
               Bill Donohoe
               John James
               Mark Peppé
               Hans Wiborg-Jenssen
               Gerald Wood

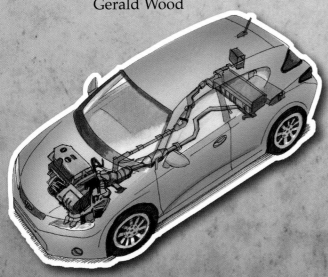

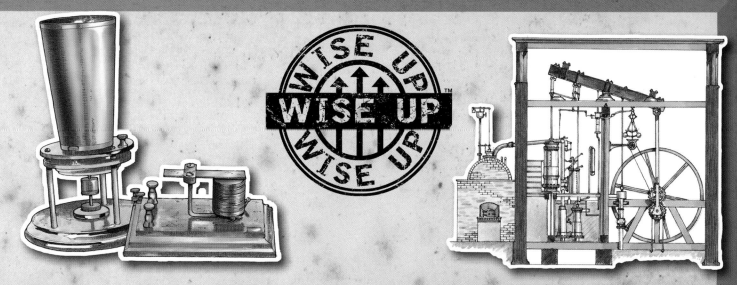

INVENTIONS

Mark Bergin

A+

Smart Apple Media

Contents

The Beginning

More than 1.5 million years ago, early humans discovered how to use sharp stones such as flints for tools and weapons. People were then able to drive off predators and hunt animals for food. Some 500,000 years ago, fire was "discovered" and used for light and warmth. Fire made meat more appetizing and safer to eat by killing off parasites and bacteria. It also made it possible to eat plants that would be inedible if uncooked.

▲ At first the only source of fire was naturally occurring, but soon people learned that friction could produce enough heat to ignite dry grass. Now humans could control fire.

◄ Writing was invented in Sumer about 3500 BCE, using a reed stylus to mark soft clay.

▲ Art was invented some 20,000 years ago when people drew on cave walls and blew natural colors onto them.

◄ Simple cloth-weaving looms date from around 7000 BCE. The loom shown here is from 1500 BCE. Threads stretched across the poles were interwoven with others at right angles.

▲ Horses, first tamed around 2000 BCE, could not be used to pull heavy loads because early harnesses could choke them. Chariots that were light enough to be pulled by horses were invented about 200 years later.

FACTFILE
STONE AGE KNIVES

• The use of stones for cutting was one of the earliest inventions. By 600,000 BCE, stones were shaped to a point or cutting edge with a rounded end to hold.

• Flint, chipped to a razor-sharp edge, was the best stone to use for tools.

The Classical Era

The achievements of Greek and Roman inventors was rarely surpassed until relatively modern times. The Greeks devised many different types of machines. Slave labor was the main source of power, so there was little incentive to develop labor-saving devices.

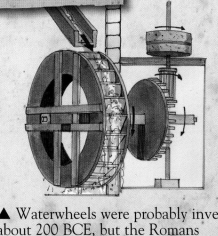

▲ Waterwheels were probably invented about 200 BCE, but the Romans normally used slaves or animal power.

▶ The Pont du Gard was built in 19 BCE. This aqueduct, about 160 feet (49 m) above the River Gardon, took water to Nîmes in southern France. It supplied every citizen with around 158 gallons (600 L) of water daily.

▲ The best Roman roads had trenches with drainage ditches at either side, a layer of sand, a layer of cement, another layer of cement with stone lumps in it, a layer of concrete topped with stone slabs or gravel, and curbstones.

▲ About 700 BCE, the Greeks invented coins. By 600 BCE the value of coins was standardized.

▲ Archimedes invented a screw to lift water from canals and rivers onto fields. It is still used in Egypt today.

The Middle Ages

The Middle Ages saw the spread of many new inventions as trade routes between Europe, Arabia, and China opened. Among the many innovations which may have come from China are stirrups, paper, gunpowder, and cannon. Arabic numerals and algebra were also introduced into medieval Europe. Water-powered mills were used to finish cloth, hammer iron, saw wood, and make paper. Mechanical technology created a medieval "industrial revolution."

◀ Spectacles were invented around 1286 CE. They were clamped onto the user's nose.

▲ The hourglass, invented in the first century CE, has remained a popular timekeeper ever since.

Su Sung's Clock

▶ Su Sung's clock of 1088 CE was driven by a waterwheel. It told the time by ringing bells and revealing small statues.

FACTFILE
LONG-LIVED CLOCK
The astronomical clock in Prague, Czech Republic, celebrated its 600th anniversary in 2010. It is the oldest working clock of its kind.

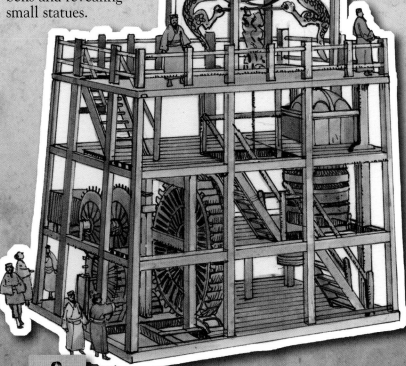

Post Mill

▶ Windmills with horizontal sails were probably invented in Persia around 700 CE. Windmills with vertical sails had been invented in Europe by 1200.

gears

hopper

▲ Gunpowder and cannon had appeared in Europe by 1346.

▲ A Chinese cannon of 1324. Gunpowder was probably discovered in China about 1000 CE.

▶ Post mills like this were widely used in the Middle Ages.

▼ The tailpole was used to turn the mill toward the wind if the wind direction changed.

tailpole

sail

millstones in wooden casing

post

trestle

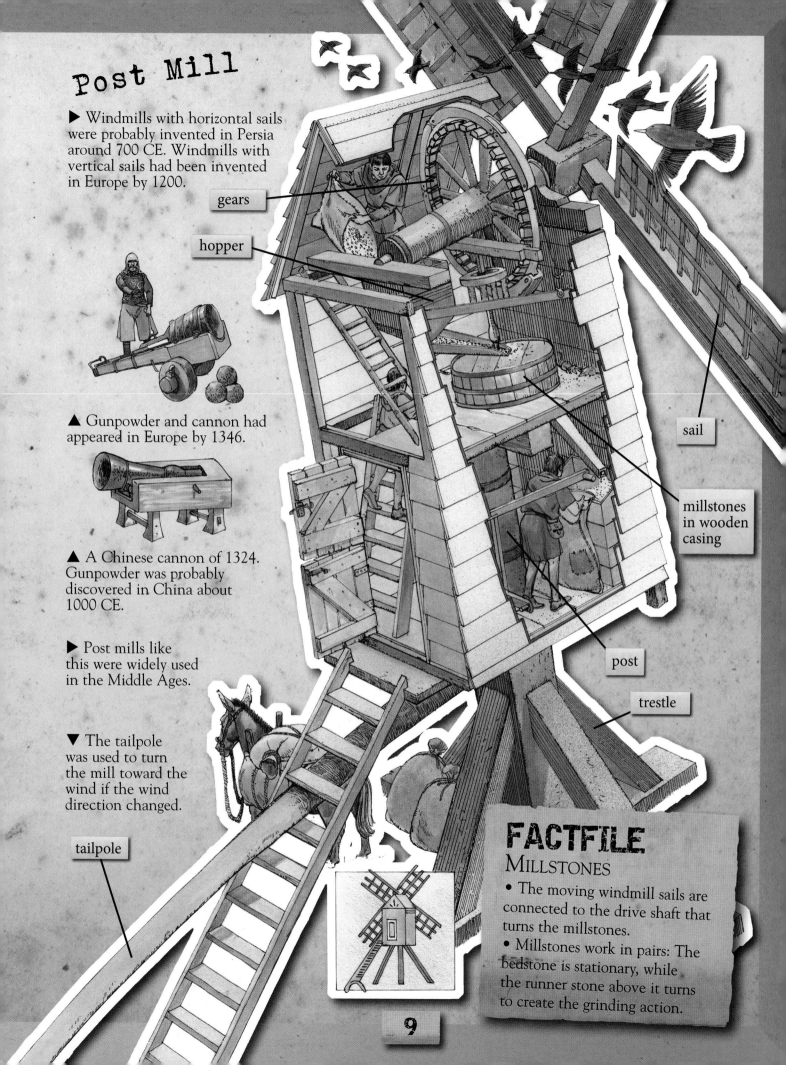

FACTFILE
MILLSTONES
• The moving windmill sails are connected to the drive shaft that turns the millstones.
• Millstones work in pairs: The bedstone is stationary, while the runner stone above it turns to create the grinding action.

The Renaissance

The Renaissance (French for "rebirth") was a time of new ideas. Scholars realized that Greek and Roman writings could be questioned, when attempts to imitate ancient technology led to new discoveries, such as drawing in perspective. The Renaissance also discovered inflation, when gold and silver from the New World poured into Europe. Surveying and mapmaking techniques improved, providing more accurate maps and charts.

Gutenberg's Press

handle

bed

The Chinese had produced printed books by 850 CE, printing each page from an individual carved wooden block. About 1200 they experimented with movable type—reusable blocks for each character—which allowed text to be built up word by word.

Movable type was impractical for the Chinese language but, by 1450, Johannes Gutenberg rediscovered it. His printing press was based on presses used for making paper or olive oil. By 1500, nearly 14,000 books had been printed.

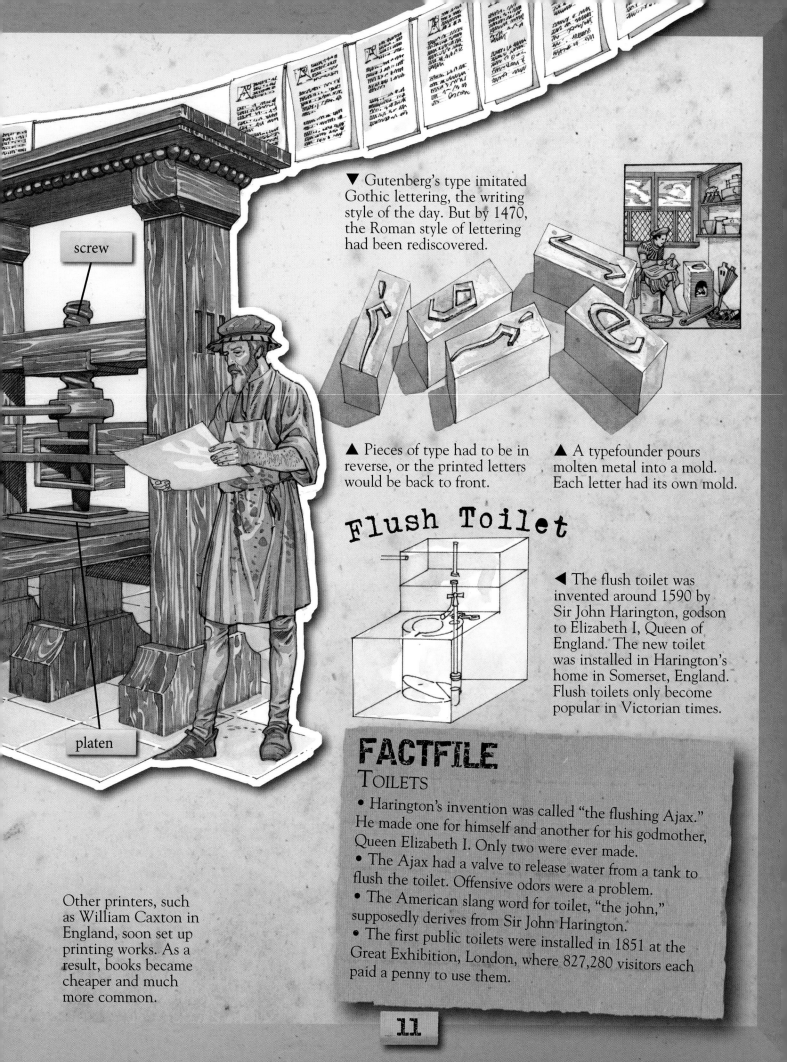

screw

platen

▼ Gutenberg's type imitated Gothic lettering, the writing style of the day. But by 1470, the Roman style of lettering had been rediscovered.

▲ Pieces of type had to be in reverse, or the printed letters would be back to front.

▲ A typefounder pours molten metal into a mold. Each letter had its own mold.

Flush Toilet

◀ The flush toilet was invented around 1590 by Sir John Harington, godson to Elizabeth I, Queen of England. The new toilet was installed in Harington's home in Somerset, England. Flush toilets only become popular in Victorian times.

FACTFILE
TOILETS

• Harington's invention was called "the flushing Ajax." He made one for himself and another for his godmother, Queen Elizabeth I. Only two were ever made.
• The Ajax had a valve to release water from a tank to flush the toilet. Offensive odors were a problem.
• The American slang word for toilet, "the john," supposedly derives from Sir John Harington.
• The first public toilets were installed in 1851 at the Great Exhibition, London, where 827,280 visitors each paid a penny to use them.

Other printers, such as William Caxton in England, soon set up printing works. As a result, books became cheaper and much more common.

The Scientific Revolution

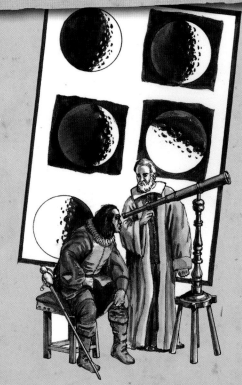

The seventeenth century saw a revolution in science, and new discoveries that would underpin the technological progress of the next few centuries. The idea that natural phenomena could be explained or described by mathematical laws was the foundation of modern physics and chemistry. In England, Sir Isaac Newton's work established gravitational theory, explaining how the universe operated. French philosopher Blaise Pascal explored the possibilities of mechanical calculation.

▲ The telescope was invented in 1608 by Hans Lippershey, a Dutch spectacle maker. He found that two lenses could make distant objects look much larger.

Calculator

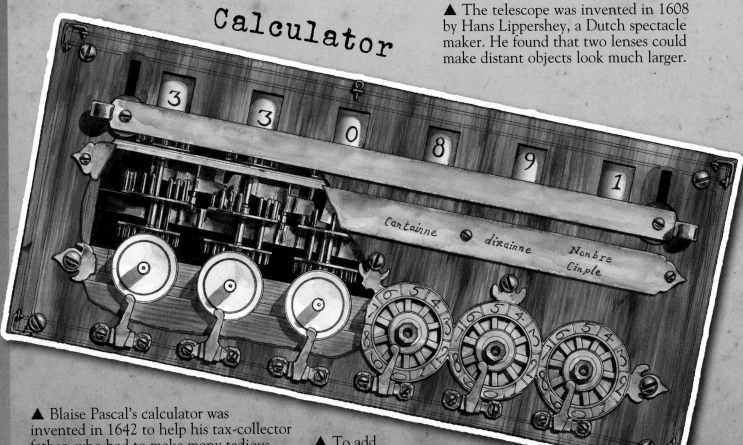

Cantainne   dixainne   Nonbre Cinple

▲ Blaise Pascal's calculator was invented in 1642 to help his tax-collector father, who had to make many tedious calculations. Pascal's first calculator took several years to build. It created great interest, but he only sold about fifteen. They were unreliable and expensive.

▲ To add numbers, the calculator wheels were turned against a pointer.

The Industrial Revolution

In the eighteenth century, Britain changed from an agricultural society into the first industrial nation. Inventions that were to transform the world were first applied in Britain during the "Industrial Revolution," from about 1760 to 1830. Improvements in agriculture meant that fewer people were needed to grow food, so more people could work in factories.

FACTFILE
SPINNING JENNY

In England, James Hargreaves invented the "spinning jenny," a machine for spinning yarn. The spinning jenny enabled one person to spin eight threads at the same time, greatly increasing productivity. It replaced the spinning wheel.

▼ The woolen mill at Bedworth, England, in the 1790s. A single waterwheel drove the machinery via a network of wooden shafts and gears.

▲ The third flight of a balloon built by the Montgolfier brothers was made in 1783. The balloon carried a rooster, a duck, and a sheep.

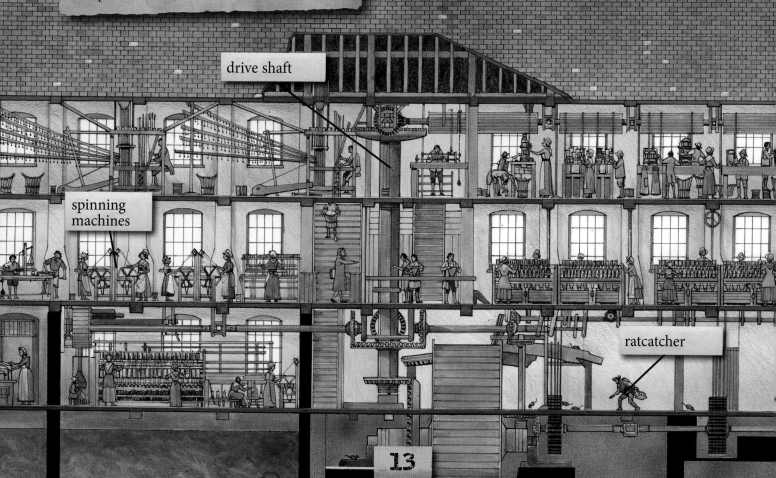

drive shaft

spinning machines

ratcatcher

The Steam Age Begins

In the eighteenth century, a new source of power was harnessed by an English inventor, Thomas Newcomen. Newcomen invented the atmospheric steam engine to pump water out of mines, to prevent the mines from flooding. The first recorded Newcomen engine, built in 1712, was used to pump out a coal mine. By the 1730s, his engines were at work in several countries, but they were not very powerful and could be used only for pumping. James Watt solved these problems. In the 1760s, he realized that Newcomen's engines were inefficient because the steam was condensed in the engine cylinder. He invented an engine with a separate condenser, followed in 1782 by an improved version which could produce rotary motion. From then on, factories did not have to rely on water power.

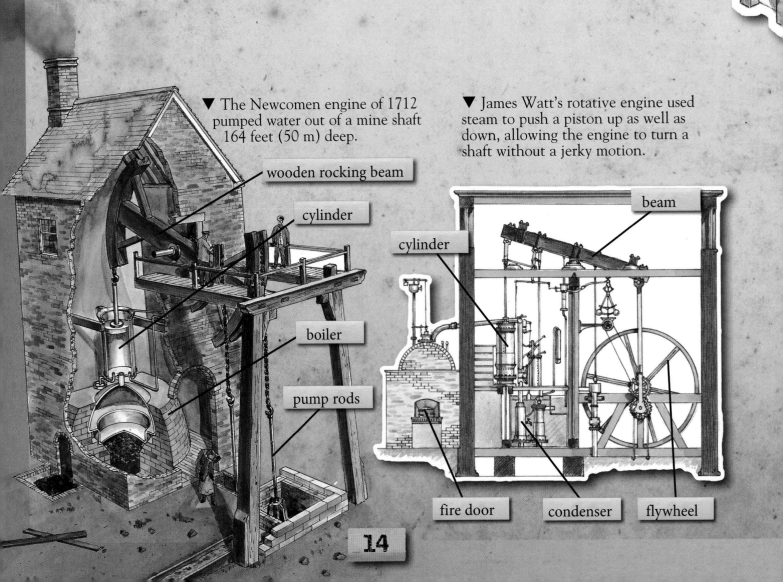

▼ The Newcomen engine of 1712 pumped water out of a mine shaft 164 feet (50 m) deep.

▼ James Watt's rotative engine used steam to push a piston up as well as down, allowing the engine to turn a shaft without a jerky motion.

wooden rocking beam

cylinder

boiler

pump rods

beam

cylinder

fire door

condenser

flywheel

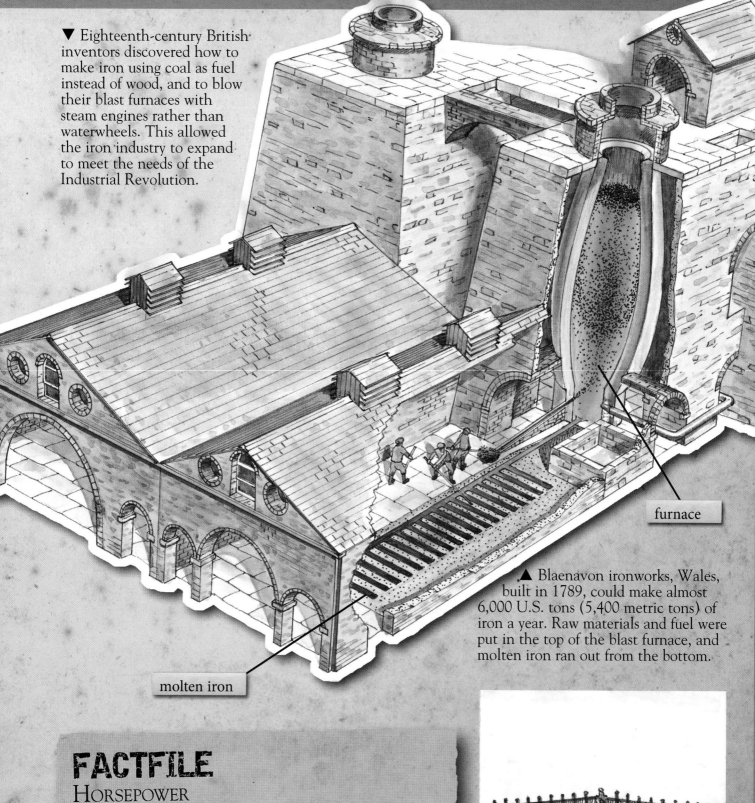

▼ Eighteenth-century British inventors discovered how to make iron using coal as fuel instead of wood, and to blow their blast furnaces with steam engines rather than waterwheels. This allowed the iron industry to expand to meet the needs of the Industrial Revolution.

furnace

molten iron

▲ Blaenavon ironworks, Wales, built in 1789, could make almost 6,000 U.S. tons (5,400 metric tons) of iron a year. Raw materials and fuel were put in the top of the blast furnace, and molten iron ran out from the bottom.

FACTFILE
HORSEPOWER

• "Horsepower" is a unit of power—a measure of the rate at which work is being done. It is most commonly used as a measure of engine output.

• In the eighteenth century, Scottish engineer James Watt used this term to compare the work power of a steam engine to that of draft horses.

▲ The first iron bridge, built in 1779 at Coalbrookdale, England.

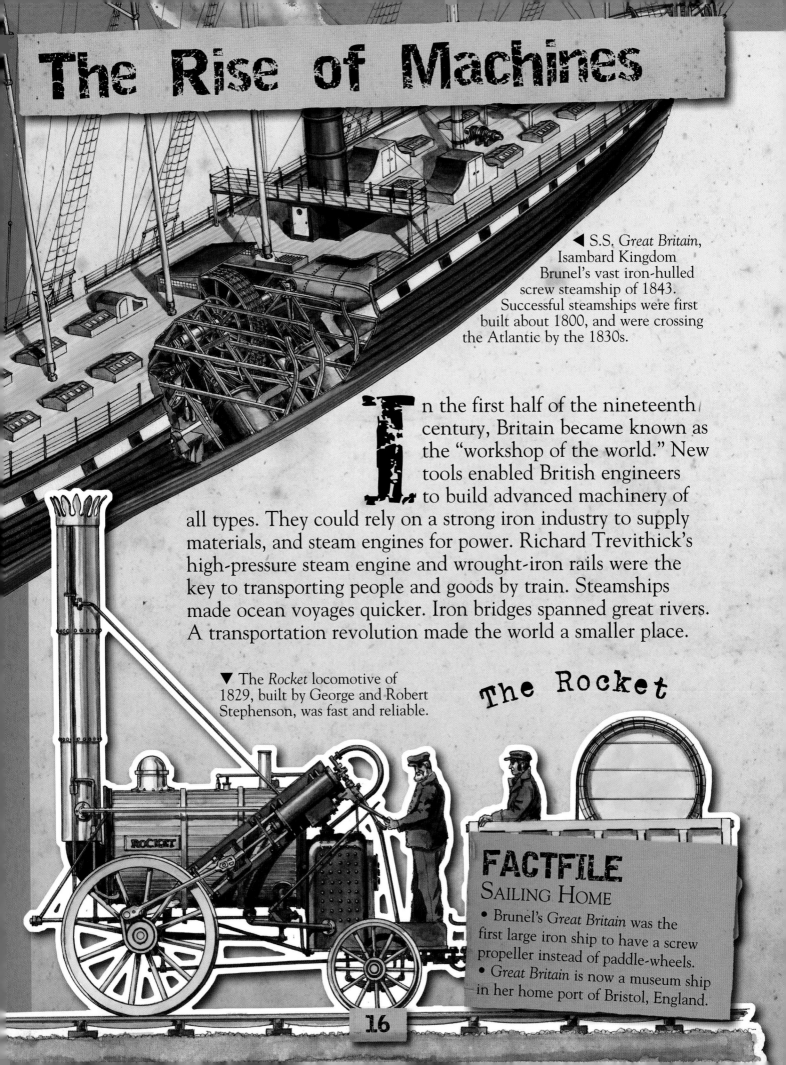

◀ S.S. *Great Britain*, Isambard Kingdom Brunel's vast iron-hulled screw steamship of 1843. Successful steamships were first built about 1800, and were crossing the Atlantic by the 1830s.

In the first half of the nineteenth century, Britain became known as the "workshop of the world." New tools enabled British engineers to build advanced machinery of all types. They could rely on a strong iron industry to supply materials, and steam engines for power. Richard Trevithick's high-pressure steam engine and wrought-iron rails were the key to transporting people and goods by train. Steamships made ocean voyages quicker. Iron bridges spanned great rivers. A transportation revolution made the world a smaller place.

▼ The *Rocket* locomotive of 1829, built by George and Robert Stephenson, was fast and reliable.

The Rocket

ROCKET

FACTFILE
SAILING HOME
• Brunel's *Great Britain* was the first large iron ship to have a screw propeller instead of paddle-wheels.
• *Great Britain* is now a museum ship in her home port of Bristol, England.

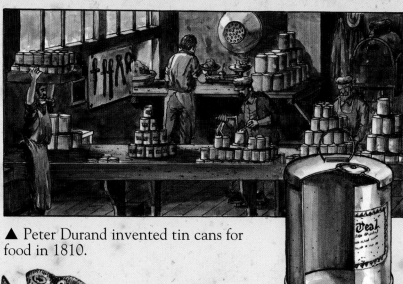

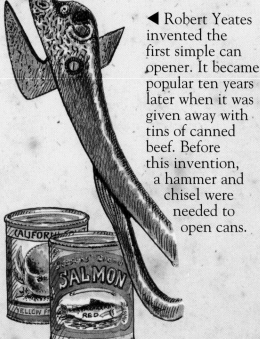

▲ Peter Durand invented tin cans for food in 1810.

◀ Robert Yeates invented the first simple can opener. It became popular ten years later when it was given away with tins of canned beef. Before this invention, a hammer and chisel were needed to open cans.

▲ Machine tools were the key to nineteenth-century technical progress. They made screws, rods, and cylinders of a size and accuracy hitherto impossible. Skilled craftsmen were replaced by machine minders, and goods could be mass-produced.

▶ The Jacquard loom was a mechanical loom programed by a sequence of punched cards to weave complex patterns automatically. Pressing the treadle moved each new card into place. This invention by Joseph-Marie Jacquard ushered in the era of automation in 1801. In the 1840s, punched cards were used to control machine tools. Later they were used to store and analyze information.

FACTFILE

COMPUTERS

Computers used punched cards until well into the 20th century.

Jacquard Loom

Electricity

Nineteenth-century scientists, exploring the properties of electricity, soon found uses for it in power, communication, and lighting. In 1821, Michael Faraday showed that it could produce rotary motion, and in 1831 he made the first electric generator. His discoveries were not widely exploited until practical generators were developed in the 1870s.

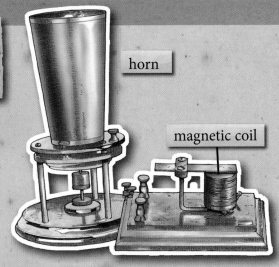

horn

magnetic coil

▲ The telephone was invented by Alexander Graham Bell in 1876. The user spoke into the horn. Magnetic coils converted the sound into electrical signals, and back again at the other end.

▶ In 1878 and 1879, both Joseph Swan and Thomas Edison invented electric lightbulbs. This created a new demand for electricity. Edison solved the problem of mass-producing lights and built the first ever power station in 1881.

▼ Edison's electric lightbulb of 1879 needed more development to find a filament that did not burn out. His notebook shows his lightbulb design.

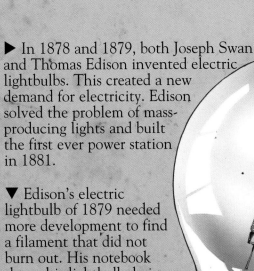

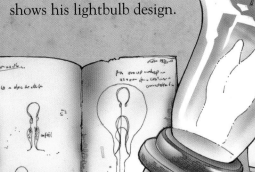

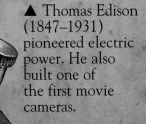

▲ Thomas Edison (1847–1931) pioneered electric power. He also built one of the first movie cameras.

▲ Radio communication grew out of the scientific discoveries of James Clerk Maxwell and Heinrich Hertz. Their work prompted the inventor Guglielmo Marconi to develop "wireless telegraphy" with his radio transmitter of 1895. By 1899, he was sending signals across the English Channel.

Urban Life

City life still depends on technologies pioneered during the nineteenth century. Clean drinking water, sewage systems, and gas and electricity supplies helped to make life healthier and more convenient. Transportation systems allowed cities to expand into modern suburbs, so people no longer had to live close to where they worked. Mass-production made a range of complicated domestic gadgets, such as sewing machines and phonographs, available at more affordable prices. Few houses yet had electric power, but inventors had grasped its possibilities for everyday living, and by 1900 electric fans, cookers, kettles, and fires were available at a price.

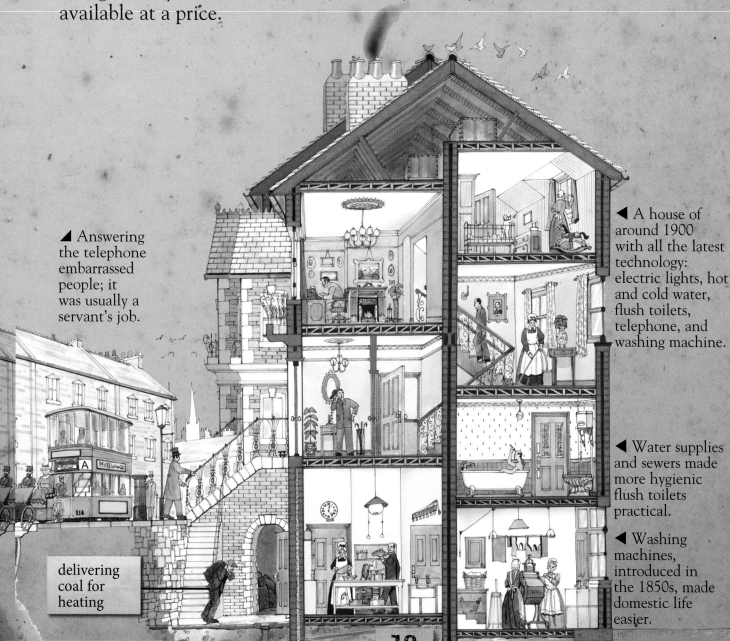

◢ Answering the telephone embarrassed people; it was usually a servant's job.

delivering coal for heating

◀ A house of around 1900 with all the latest technology: electric lights, hot and cold water, flush toilets, telephone, and washing machine.

◀ Water supplies and sewers made more hygienic flush toilets practical.

◀ Washing machines, introduced in the 1850s, made domestic life easier.

Medicine

Medical progress was rapid during the nineteenth century. Many of the tools developed during this period are still in use today. In the 1840s, safe anesthetics were first used, banishing pain from the operating theater. By 1862, Louis Pasteur had shown that many diseases were caused by germs.

Lister's Carbolic Spray

Smallpox

▲ Edward Jenner was the first to use vaccination, against smallpox.

▶ Robert Koch in 1882 isolated the germ that causes tuberculosis.

▲ Joseph Lister introduced antiseptic surgery, using disinfectant, in 1867. Lister's carbolic acid spray was pumped over surgeons and patient.

▼ Blood transfusions were often fatal, until blood groups were discovered by Karl Landsteiner in 1900.

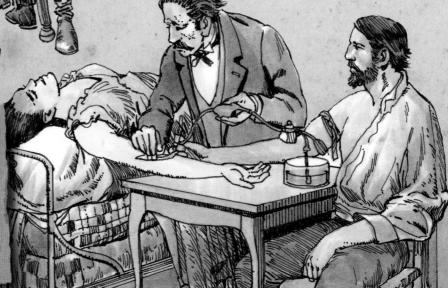

FACTFILE
MEDICAL INVENTIONS
- 1847: Anesthetic inhaler
- ca. 1855: Stethoscope
- ca. 1865: Medical thermometers
- ca. 1887: Sphygmomanometer
(for measuring blood pressure)

Steel and Aluminum

Steel was the hardest and strongest metal known, but it was expensive to make until Sir Henry Bessemer invented the first bulk steelmaking process in 1856. The Siemens–Martin process followed in 1863, and engineers began using steel for railroad rails, larger ships and bridges, and long-lasting machine parts. Alloy steelmaking, pioneered by David Mushet in 1868, made it possible to develop steels for different applications.

▲ In the Bessemer converter, air was blown through molten iron, turning it into steel.

The Forth Bridge

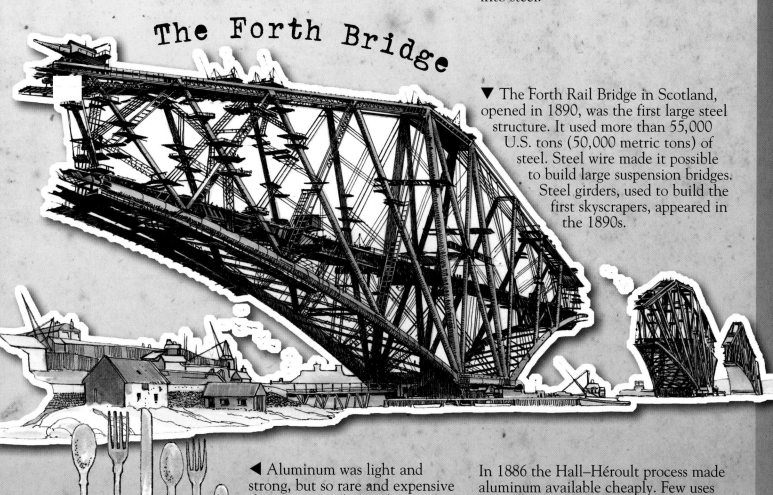

▼ The Forth Rail Bridge in Scotland, opened in 1890, was the first large steel structure. It used more than 55,000 U.S. tons (50,000 metric tons) of steel. Steel wire made it possible to build large suspension bridges. Steel girders, used to build the first skyscrapers, appeared in the 1890s.

◀ Aluminum was light and strong, but so rare and expensive that it was used to make jewelry. French emperor Napoleon III had his best cutlery made from aluminum.

In 1886 the Hall–Héroult process made aluminum available cheaply. Few uses were found for it at first, but aluminum was to become vital for aircraft parts in the future.

Travel in the 20th Century

T he airplane was one of the most significant inventions of the twentieth century; it was to revolutionize both transportation and warfare.

Radio communication went from strength to strength; in 1901 it spanned the Atlantic, and ship-to-shore radio ended the age-old isolation of the mariner. The turbine, a new type of steam engine invented in 1884 by Charles Parsons, was being rapidly adopted to generate electricity and power ships, and the motor car became a practical means of transport.

▲ Count Zeppelin built the first successful airship in 1900.

Ford Model T

▶ Henry Ford's mass-production techniques lowered car prices. When Ford Model T production lines closed in 1927, over 15 million cars had been made.

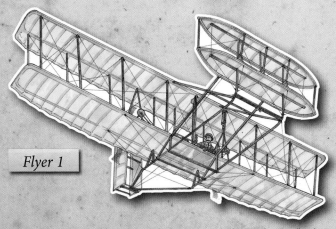

Flyer 1

▲ Orville Wright made the first powered airplane flight at Kitty Hawk, North Carolina, in 1903 with his brother, Wilbur, running alongside. The 12-second flight covered 120 feet (37 m). Later that day, they achieved a 59-second flight covering 852 feet (260 m).

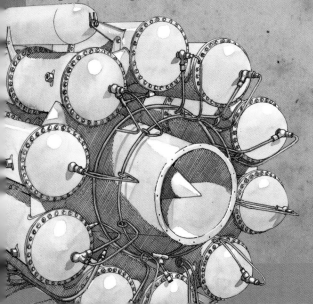

◀ An engine similar to this powered the first British jet plane in 1941. The jet engine was developed simultaneously in Britain and Germany, by Frank Whittle and Hans von Ohain.

FACTFILE
THE WRIGHT FLYER

Flyer 1 had two wings 39 feet (12 m) across. The pilot controlled ascent and descent using the elevator, the small front wing. The aircraft was turned by twisting the main wings and turning the rudders at the back of the craft.

▶ A hybrid electric car. The electric motor improves fuel economy and performance. First invented by Ferdinand Porsche in 1901, the technology became widely available with Toyota's Prius of 1997. More than 3,000,000 of these had been sold by 2013.

lift-off hood

fender

radiator

engine

right-hand steering

The Channel Tunnel opened in 1994. The train journey from London to Paris takes 2 hours 15 minutes.

Space Shuttle

FACTFILE
SHUTTLE MISSIONS
- Between 1981 and 2011, Kennedy Space Center, Florida, launched 135 Shuttle missions.
- There were six space shuttles: *Enterprise*, *Columbia*, *Challenger*, *Discovery*, *Atlantis*, and *Endeavour*.
- The Space Shuttle program came to an end on July 21, 2011.

▲ NASA's Space Shuttle made its first flight in 1981. The Shuttle program lasted 30 years, despite two fatal accidents. In 1986 the shuttle *Challenger* exploded soon after its launch, and in 2003 the shuttle *Columbia* was destroyed during re-entry. The four surviving shuttles are now preserved in various museums in the United States.

At Home in the 20ᵗʰ Century

During the 1920s, speech transmission by radio made public broadcasting possible, opening up a new world of home entertainment. The first public broadcasts were made in 1920, by the Marconi Company in England and the Westinghouse Company in the United States.

Electric refrigerators, hair dryers, and food mixers all became available around this time.

▼ An A.J.S. valve radio receiver of 1923, with an S. G. Brown horn loudspeaker. Early valve radios were expensive and difficult to operate.

◢ John Logie Baird's mechanical television system. Light from the object being televised passed through a rotating disc with a spiral of holes in it, and on to a photocell that converted it into an electrical signal. The signal was broadcast to the receiver, where it lit a bulb that shone light through another disc and onto a screen, producing a picture of the object.

▼ The safety razor with disposable blades was invented by King Camp Gillette in 1901. He wanted to invent something that could only be used once, then thrown away and replaced. By 1906, 90,000 razors and 12,400,000 blades had been sold.

Razor

▼ Plasma TV: This 1997 model with a 42-inch (107-cm) screen offered improved brightness and contrast.

▶ Modern households aim to use as little energy as possible. This compact fluorescent lightbulb from 1991 uses only 18 watts of electricity, but gives as much light as an ordinary 60-watt bulb. It is claimed to last 12,000 hours or 11 years.

▲ Some of our electricity is now generated from renewable sources, such as wind turbines and solar panels. Wind turbines are often grouped in large arrays called wind farms. Solar panels can be small enough to fit on the roof of an ordinary house.

The Electronic Age

Many long-popular technologies are now almost obsolete. The incandescent light bulb is being phased out globally in favor of energy-efficient alternatives. Digital cameras have virtually taken over the camera market to replace film-based photography and cinematography. Computers, Internet access, and e-books have overtaken traditional sources of information such as books and newspapers, making the survival of public libraries questionable.

▲ By 2008, 1 billion personal computers were in use. The DVD was invented in 1996 and has transformed the way we watch television.

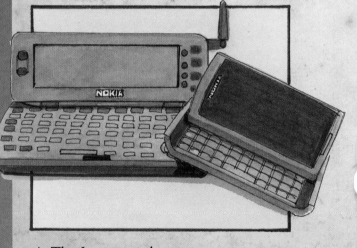

▲ The Internet is becoming more mobile all the time. The Nokia 9000 Communicator of 1996 weighed 14 ounces (397 g). The 2011 Nokia E7 smartphone weighed just over 6 ounces (176 g).

▶ The Kodak Digital Camera System (1991–2005) was designed to replace professional film cameras.

shoulder pack with battery charger

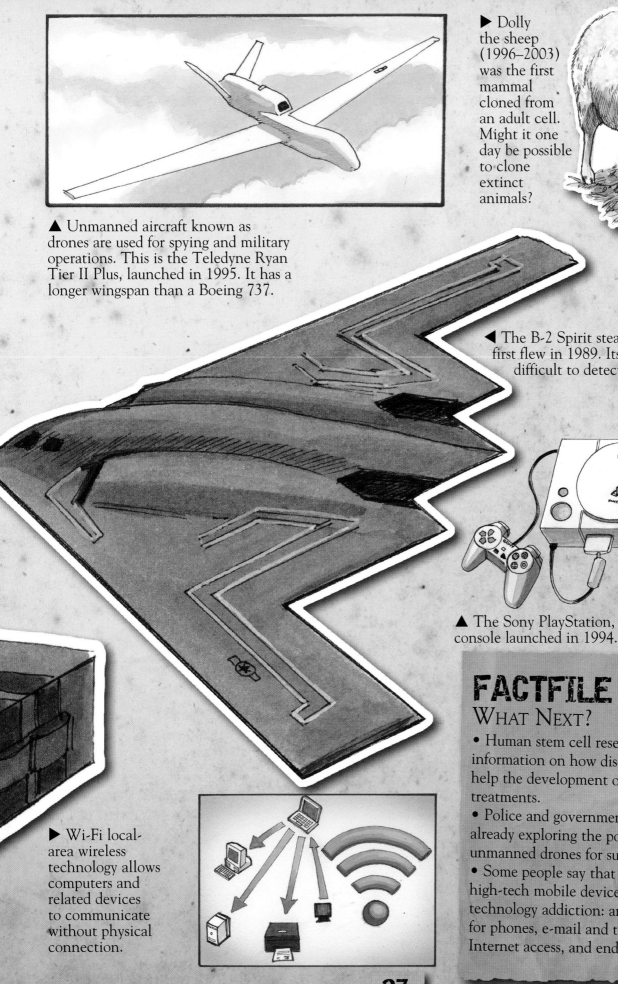

▲ Unmanned aircraft known as drones are used for spying and military operations. This is the Teledyne Ryan Tier II Plus, launched in 1995. It has a longer wingspan than a Boeing 737.

▶ Dolly the sheep (1996–2003) was the first mammal cloned from an adult cell. Might it one day be possible to clone extinct animals?

◀ The B-2 Spirit stealth bomber first flew in 1989. Its shape makes it difficult to detect with radar.

▲ The Sony PlayStation, a games console launched in 1994.

▶ Wi-Fi local-area wireless technology allows computers and related devices to communicate without physical connection.

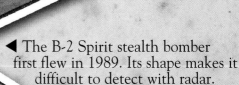

FACTFILE
WHAT NEXT?

• Human stem cell research should yield information on how diseases arise, to help the development of future cures and treatments.

• Police and government agencies are already exploring the potential of using unmanned drones for surveillance.

• Some people say that the use of high-tech mobile devices is creating technology addiction: an incessant need for phones, e-mail and texting facilities, Internet access, and endless photography.

Into the Future

Technology now evolves and becomes redundant at a much faster pace. Miraculous inventions already in development include 3-D printers; smart contact lenses to help people with diabetes to monitor their blood glucose level; self-driving cars; "bionic eye" implants; food created from stem cells; and manned travel to Mars.

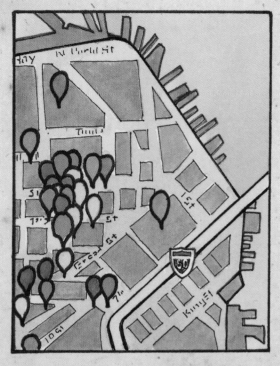

▼ *SpaceShipOne* first flew in 2003. It was launched from the mother ship, *White Knight*, in 2004 in the first private, manned space flight.

◄ Apple's first smartphone was released in 2007. The App Store followed in 2008.

▲ Google Maps is a desktop and cell-phone mapping service first released in 2005. It offers satellite images, street maps, and street-level views.

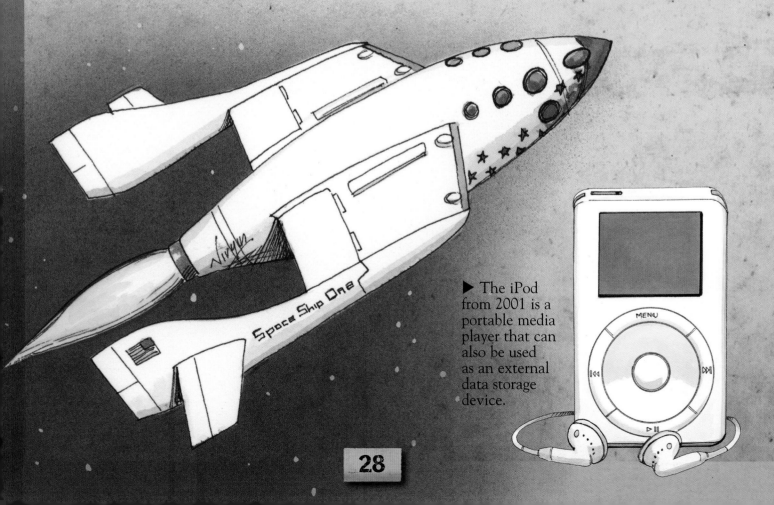

► The iPod from 2001 is a portable media player that can also be used as an external data storage device.

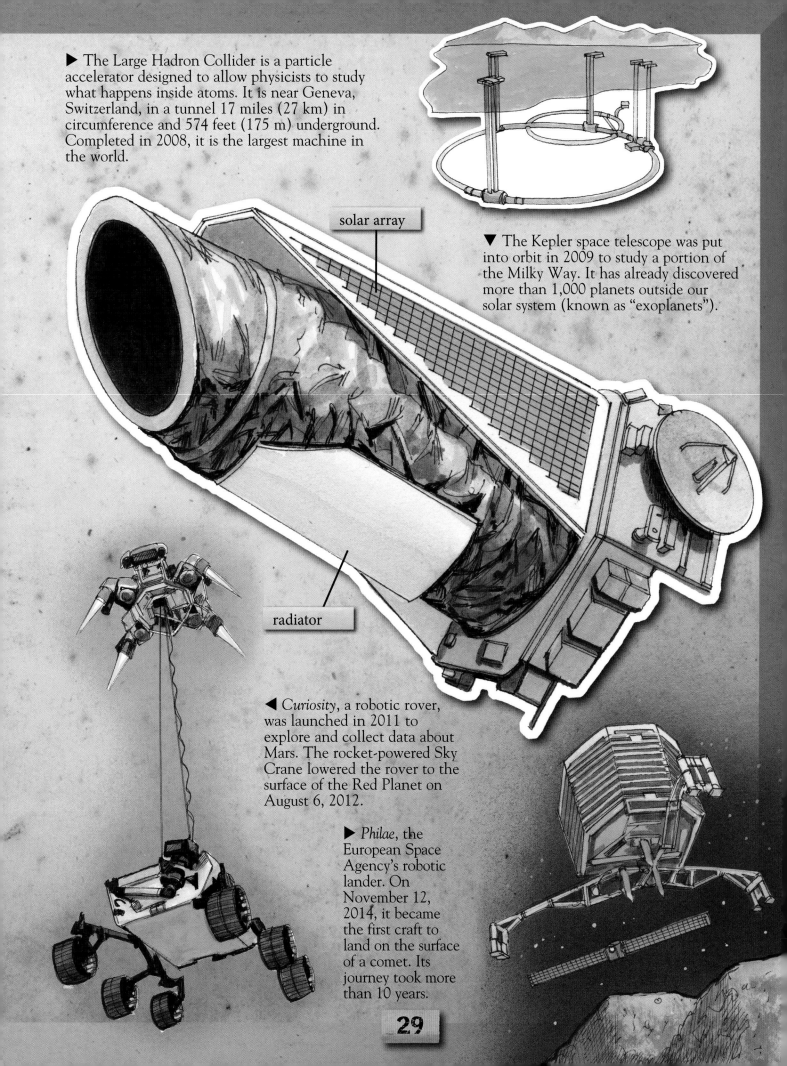

▶ The Large Hadron Collider is a particle accelerator designed to allow physicists to study what happens inside atoms. It is near Geneva, Switzerland, in a tunnel 17 miles (27 km) in circumference and 574 feet (175 m) underground. Completed in 2008, it is the largest machine in the world.

solar array

▼ The Kepler space telescope was put into orbit in 2009 to study a portion of the Milky Way. It has already discovered more than 1,000 planets outside our solar system (known as "exoplanets").

radiator

◀ *Curiosity*, a robotic rover, was launched in 2011 to explore and collect data about Mars. The rocket-powered Sky Crane lowered the rover to the surface of the Red Planet on August 6, 2012.

▶ *Philae*, the European Space Agency's robotic lander. On November 12, 2014, it became the first craft to land on the surface of a comet. Its journey took more than 10 years.

Inventions Quiz

1. What was James Hargreaves's spinning machine called?
a) The spinning jimmy
b) The flywheel
c) The spinning jenny

2. What did Archimedes invent?
a) The first writing system
b) A labor-saving device to lift water from rivers
c) The printing press

3. Who invented television?
a) Henry Ford
b) John Logie Baird
c) Blaise Pascal

4. The Large Hadron Collider is the biggest machine in the world. What country is it in?
a) Switzerland
b) Italy
c) Germany

5. Who invented the telescope ?
a) Hans Lippershey
b) Thomas Edison
c) Johannes Gutenberg

6. In which year was Stephenson's *Rocket* locomotive built?
a) 1903
b) 1829
c) 1867

7. When was the flush toilet invented?
a) 1870s
b) 1590s
c) 1920s

8. What was the name of the Wright Brothers' first airplane?
a) *Flyer 1*
b) *Airplane 1*
c) *Biplane 1*

9. What did Karl Landsteiner discover?
a) Antiseptic surgery
b) Different blood groups
c) Gunpowder

10. How long did the European Space Agency's *Philae* lander take to reach its destination comet?
a) About 6 weeks
b) 322 days 7 hrs 20 m
c) More than 10 years

Quiz answers

1) c see page 13
2) b see page 7
3) b see page 24
4) a see page 29
5) a see page 12
6) b see page 16
7) b see page 11
8) a see page 22
9) b see page 20
10) c see page 29

Glossary

anesthetic A drug that prevents patients from feeling pain, especially during a surgical operation.

aqueduct A man-made channel for carrying water from a lake or spring to the place where it is needed.

astronomical clock A clock that shows the movements of the sun, moon, and zodiac signs.

blast furnace A chamber in which ore (rock containing useful minerals) is heated to extract the minerals from it.

clone To make copies of living cells by artificial means.

condense To change from a gas or vapor (such as steam) into a liquid (such as water).

exoplanet A planet outside our own solar system.

extinct Having died out completely.

filament A thin metal wire that glows when heated, used in incandescent lightbulbs.

friction The rubbing of one surface against another.

hybrid Something that is a mixture of two different things, such as a car that has both an electric motor and a gasoline engine.

incandescent bulb The older type of lightbulb, in which a metal filament glows when heated by an electric current.

Industrial Revolution The period in the late 18th and early 19th centuries when many new technologies were developed.

inflation A general increase in prices.

medieval Belonging to the Middle Ages, the period from ca. 1000 CE

(or earlier) to ca. 1500 CE.

molten Melted into a liquid.

NASA The National Aeronautics and Space Administration, the United States government agency for space exploration.

particle accelerator A machine that moves tiny fragments of matter at extremely high speeds, to help scientists study what happens inside atoms.

phonograph A machine for recording sounds on a wax cylinder and playing them back.

photocell A device that produces an electric current when exposed to light.

predator An animal that hunts other animals for food.

redundant No longer needed.

re-entry The return of a spacecraft into Earth's atmosphere. The friction of the atmosphere against the craft generates heat, which may damage the spacecraft.

renewable energy Energy obtained from sources that will always be available—such as the sun, wind, and waves—as opposed to oil, coal, or gas, which will eventually be used up.

rotative engine An engine that turns the up-and-down movement of a piston inside a cylinder into the turning movement of a wheel.

stem cell A special type of cell in the body that can develop into different kinds of cells. Scientists study these cells in the hope of finding new treatments for diseases.

stylus A pointed tool used to make

marks in a soft material, such as clay or wax.

Sumer A Bronze Age civilisation of the Middle East, in an area that is now part of southern Iraq. It flourished from ca. 5300 BCE to ca. 2300 BCE.

telegraphy Sending signals or messages over long distances.

tuberculosis A serious disease for which there was no cure until antibiotics (medicines that kill germs) were discovered.

turbine A device resembling a propeller that spins, generating energy, when a liquid or gas passes through its blades.

vaccination A method of preventing disease by giving the patient a weakened form of the disease so that the body can build up its own defenses against that particular disease.

Index